Text copyright © 1988 by Barbara Steiner
Illustrations copyright © 1988 by Gretchen Will Mayo

First published in the United States of America in 1988 by Walker Publishing Company, Inc.; first paperback edition published in 1995.

Published simultaneously in Canada by Thomas Allen & Son Canada, Limited, Markham, Ontario.

The Library of Congress cataloged the hardcover editions of this book as follows:
Steiner, Barbara
   Whale brother / by Barbara Steiner : illustrations by Gretchen Will Mayo.
   p.   cm.
   Summary: Omu longs to find the magic he needs to create great whalebone carvings and inspired music on his harmonica, but he does not discover the inspiration until he stands watch beside a dying killer whale.
   ISBN 0-8027-6804-0. — ISBN 8027-6805-9 (lib. bdg.)
   1. Eskimos—Juvenile fiction. 2. Indians of North America—Juvenile fiction. (1. Eskimos—Fiction. 2. Indians of North America—Fiction. 3. Killer whale—Fiction. 4. Whales—Fiction. 5. Artists—Fiction.) I. Mayo, Gretchen, ill. II. Title.
PZ7.S825Wh 1988
(E)—dc19   88-5565
                                                    CIP
                                                    AC

ISBN 0-8027-7460-1 (paper)

Text design by Laurie McBarnette

Printed in China

10 9 8 7 6

For the mighty killer whale, the great Skana, who instills fear and awe into man. May his brother-man regard him with admiration, let him live, and be joyful.

Thank you for inspiration to Joan McIntyre, who understands the bond between man and whale, whale and man.

—B.S.

For Tom

—G.W.M.

Whale
Brother

Barbara Steiner

Illustrations by Gretchen Will Mayo

Walker and Company
New York

Omu took his best whalebone carving to show his father. He wanted his father to be proud of him.

"This is a good seal," said Omu's father. "Someday you can be as great an artist as Padloq. But your seal has no life."

"How can I make this bone come alive?" asked Omu. "That's not possible."

"I do not know," said Father. "I am a hunter, not a carver."

Omu went to Padloq. The carver took Omu's seal. "This looks like a seal, but it has no spirit. You must learn to see the seal in the bone. Then you set it free when you carve. Sometimes you wait many days before the seal is born. This stillness is called *qarrtsiluni*—waiting for something to burst."

Omu looked at Padloq's carving. Padloq's white bear smiled at Omu. He picked up a piece of bone. He saw nothing in it to set free. How long did one have to wait?

Sitting on a rock, Omu watched gulls wheel and dip. He thought and waited. He waited and thought. No answers came. Then he heard the boys calling.

"The trader is coming!

"The trader is coming!"

Omu longed for a harmonica from the trader's pack. It had a silver jacket and many notes. Maybe Omu would not be a carver. He would be a musician. He offered the trader his seal.

The trader turned the carving over and over. "This piece is not good enough. What else do you have to trade?"

Omu was disappointed. Even the trader could see his work was not good.

"What about that spear?" asked the trader. "I'll give you the harmonica for your spear."

Omu hadn't thought of trading his spear. His father had made it, and Omu felt proud to carry it. But he wanted the harmonica.

"All right." Slowly Omu handed the trader his spear. When he held the harmonica, he felt better. He forgot his spear. He forgot his carving. He forgot his problem of making a bone come alive.

At first Omu could play only *whooo* and *whaaa*. But he knew if he practiced he could make beautiful songs. He played instead of carving.

"Get out of this igloo with your noises," said Father one day.

Omu didn't want his father angry, so he hid and practiced until the other boys found him. They taunted and tattled.

"Omu is no musician.

"Omu is no carver.

"Omu is no hunter, since he gave away his spear.

"Omu is an old woman who hides to make funny noises."

When they moved for the summer, Father would not let Omu play his harmonica in the skin tent. "First you gave away your spear for that toy. Now you've become a waster of days."

Omu felt sad. Father didn't understand. He wanted Omu to be a carver. He couldn't understand that Omu didn't know how to find the animals in the bone.

Omu hid the beautiful harmonica. He was afraid Father would lose patience and take it. He did not play his music. He did not carve. He did nothing.

"Do something, you lazy boy!" Father said. "Go fishing. Maybe you can catch some fish."

Omu got in his kayak. Soon he found an inlet that led to a quiet spoon-bowl of water. Instead of fishing, Omu let his kayak drift. He took out his harmonica and played. After several hours a song of many notes came from the silver harmonica.

When Omu returned home without fish, Father said, "You are useless to your family. You are useless to the tribe. I am ashamed of you."

Omu's heart was heavy. Only when he was alone, playing his music, did he feel good. So, early each morning, he paddled to his secret place.

One day, when the Sun Sister was beaming light on the water, Omu looked up. Five black sails swished in a circle around his kayak. *Killer whales!* His heart pounded.

But he kept playing. The whales seemed to dance to his music. They filled the air with singing. Then the five whales stood on their tails side by side.

Omu laughed out loud. Quickly he made up a lively tune called "I Spy."

I spy you in the water, standing.
You see me sitting in my skin-boat body.
I play my strange and beautiful music.
You listen and dance in the water.
You sing your song of the seas.
We no longer fear each other.
The music makes us brothers.

Splash! The whales leapt back into the water.
Swish! They swam in circles.
Swoosh! They breathed together.

Each night Omu paddled home. He told no one of his friends. He spent each day with his whale brothers. He played them songs for hunting. He played them songs for swimming.

Songs for dancing.

Songs for leaping.

And they sang their songs for him.

One day Omu entered the narrow handle of water. He paddled into the spoon-bowl. He could see no black sails. Had his friends returned to the ocean?

Shading his eyes, he looked in all directions. On one shore he saw something wrong. Quickly he paddled toward it.

Skana, the great male, was lying on the shore.

"Why do you lie there on land, O great friend? You belong in the water."

Skana looked at Omu with large, sad eyes, but he could not move.

Skana's family surfaced to circle Omu's kayak. Their song was mournful. Omu felt their sadness on his heart.

Omu paddled up to the beach and pulled the kayak onto the sand. He pushed and tugged at the great whale. "I cannot help, my friend."

Omu stroked the whale's head, touching him as he would a brother. Skana's skin was dry and dull. Omu filled his pouch with water and poured it over the great Skana until the whale glistened.

Then he sat beside his whale brother and played his harmonica to ease the pain.

O Sedna, why do you not want Skana in the sea?
Why have you caused him to be unlucky?
He loved the water, O Sedna.
He loved his family.
He spent long hours teaching his children to live in the ocean.
He was a good hunter.
Why have you caused him to be unlucky?

Next Omu played a happy song of racing through the great seas. Of diving and splashing. Of sounding deep into dark waters and shooting up with a burst of bubbles.

Aja, the sea is lovely.
The waters touch my body, making me slick and beautiful.
Aja, I play like a happy child with my family.
Aja, I am free.
I fear no enemy.
I am a fine hunter.
I teach my children about the great waters.
Aja, I am a brother to the sea.

For five days and nights Omu sat with his whale brother, singing and playing his harmonica. He did not listen to the rumble of his stomach. He did not listen for the sorrowing of his mother who would think Omu lost.

He sat through the short nights when the Moon Brother painted the waters silver.

He told Skana of the dancing spirits on the horizon around the fires of heaven.

He sat through the long days when the Sun Sister beamed light at every corner of their world.

Near the shore, Skana's family kept watch. They whistled their love and respect. They told Skana of their sadness and how they missed him in the water.

Omu knew one of the whales was Skana's son. Omu thought of his own father. He knew some day his father would go to the land of the Souls.

In the early dawn a whale tossed Omu a walrus tusk of ivory. Omu took out his knife and began to carve. He told his whale brother how beautiful he was, and how beautiful the ivory. He asked Skana's spirit to come into the ivory as he carved.

All day he worked carefully as he talked to the great Skana. He would look for the killer whale in the ivory. He would set it free.

The killer whale, I carve it.
It is like the beautiful Skana.
I carve him mighty as the seas.
I carve him strong as the white bear.
I carve him brave as the shaman.
I carve him shiny as the Moon Brother.
I carve him happy as the dolphin.
I carve him sad as his Omu.
He shall go home to live with the Great Spirits.

It was over. The great Skana gave up his life in Omu's world. Omu played a happy song on his harmonica for the soul of Skana to fly to the Spirit World.

Go, Great Whale,
To the land of the Souls.
May your spirit dance in the sea,
Calling out greetings,
Sending good luck to your family,
To your Omu.
Protect your Omu.
Give him good carvings.
Give him your joy of the oceans.
Give him your luck in hunting.
You have left on a fine day.
I have great sorrow.
I have great joy.

Omu's mother and father were waiting on the shore.

"Every day we looked. We thought you had gone to live with the Great Spirits."

"I'm sorry you worried, but I had to stay with my friend." Omu told them about Skana. He showed them the ivory carving that held the spirit of the great whale.

"This is a fine carving, my son. You have worked carefully. You took time to find the life in the ivory."

"The whale is my brother," said Omu. "He came into my work."

Omu played the songs he had played for the killer whale. Then quickly he made up a song about his joy at being home. The music made his mother laugh.

"You have found many songs in that harmonica," Father said. "I know now that you needed your music too."

It had taken time for Omu to find the songs in the harmonica and it took time to set the carvings free. He had found the time it takes to wait for the stillness, the *qarrtsiluni*.